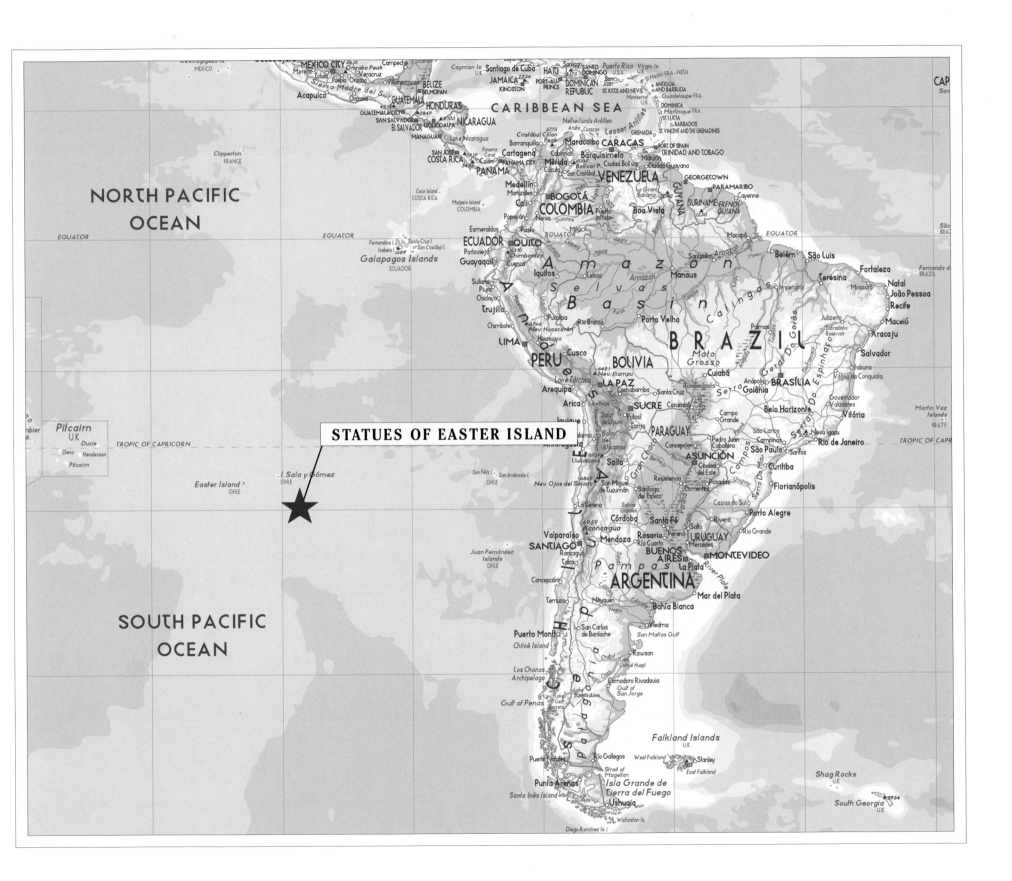

Published by Creative Education
123 South Broad Street
Mankato, Minnesota 56001

Creative Education is an imprint of The Creative Company.

Designed by Stephanie Blumenthal
Production design by The Design Lab
Art direction by Rita Marshall

Photographs by Corbis (James L. Amos, Bernard Annebicque, Yann Arthus-Bertrand,
Bettmann, Christie's Images, Stephanie Colasanti, Paul Edmondson, Ric Ergenbright,
Kevin Fleming, Owen Franken, Farrell Grehan, Hulton-Deutsch Collection, Images.com,
Wolfgang Kaehler, Catherine Karnow, Richard T. Nowitz, Douglas Peebles, Kevin Schafer,
Leonard de Selva, Hubert Stadler, Stapleton Collection, Hans Strand, Steve Terrill,
Stuart Westmorland, Adam Woolfitt)

Printed in the United States of America

Library of Congress Cataloging-in-Publication Data

Franzen, Lenore.
Statues of Easter Island / by Lenore Franzen.
p. cm. — (Ancient wonders of the world)
Includes index.
ISBN 1-58341-358-8
1. Prehistoric peoples—Easter Island. 2. Sculpture, Prehistoric—Easter Island.
3. Polynesians—Easter Island—Antiquities. 4. Easter Island—Antiquities.
I. Title. II. Series.

F3169.F73 2005   961'.8—dc22   2004055267

First edition

2 4 6 8 9 7 5 3 1

Statues of
Easter Island

LENORE FRANZEN

CREATIVE 🍎 EDUCATION

Framed by the bright blue sky and deep blue sea, the statues of Easter Island are an impressive reminder of the power of an ancient society.

Winds always blow there. Waves pound the rugged coastline. For millions of years, only seabirds and dragonflies occupied this 64-square-mile (163 sq km) triangle of land in the middle of the Pacific Ocean, more than 1,000 miles (1,600 km) from the nearest inhabited island. But for the last 1,600 years, the island has also been home to hundreds of massive stone statues keeping silent watch over the grassy landscape and fields of hardened black lava. The angular faces and deep-set eyes of these figures have long intrigued explorers and **archaeologists** hoping to unlock the mysteries surrounding perhaps the loneliest place on Earth—Easter Island.

4

STONE SPIRITS

Because Easter Island is so isolated, the Rapa Nui had to be self-sufficient. They raised roosters (below) and grew sweet potatoes (opposite top left), sugar cane (opposite top right), bananas (opposite bottom left), and gourds (opposite bottom right). They also used totora reeds as thatch for their houses (right).

Easter Island, Hawaii, and New Zealand together form the Polynesian Triangle. Within this area lie all of the islands on which Polynesian people live. As early as 5500 B.C., people in East Polynesia were moving about in wooden canoes, trading in obsidian—a hard, glass-like rock—and gradually moving west. In about A.D. 400, a small group of these seafarers came upon the island that would later be named Easter Island. The Rapa Nui, as the people were called, brought plants and animals with them—including sweet potatoes, bottle gourds, totora reeds, and chickens—

and began a new life on the previously uninhabited dot of land.

The Rapa Nui were skilled sculptors, and during the next 800 to 1,300 years, they fashioned nearly 900 stone statues, or *moai* (pronounced mo-EYE), out of volcanic rock. The Rapa Nui erected nearly a third of them around the island, particularly along the coasts. Large statues were carved on other Polynesian islands as well, but none as large or numerous as those on Easter Island.

The *moai* are believed to represent the spirits of chiefs or other high-ranking

6

At one time, more than 40 varieties of yams and 25 varieties of sweet potatoes were grown on Easter Island. Sweet potatoes in particular served as fuel for the Rapa Nui workers who carved, transported, and erected the *moai*.

During the 1700s, the people of Easter Island worshipped Makemake, a god who was half man, half bird. In a contest held every year, young men swam to a rock outcropping a half-mile (805 m) from shore, captured the egg of the sooty tern, and brought it to their clan leader. The first leader to receive the egg became the symbolic birdman for that year.

Some moai *are partly buried in hillsides (opposite), while others stand erect along the coast (right).*

ancestors of a family or clan. Like other Polynesian societies, the Rapa Nui believed that people's **lineage** defined their place in life. The *moai*, then, were **icons** for those individuals who ranked at the top of their group. When the Rapa Nui gathered for religious ceremonies and rituals, they worshipped their gods through the towering *moai* that seemed to hold up the sky. The great statues linked sky and earth, gods and chiefs, and chiefs and people.

On the eastern side of Easter Island is a quarry called Rano Raraku; it was here that most of the statues were carved. More than 70 percent of the *moai* hauled out of the quarry were raised onto *ahu*, stone platforms built along the island's coasts. These platforms marked the site where clans held various religious ceremonies. Archaeologists have identified more than 245 *ahu* on Easter Island; most are near the island's black lava cliffs, which rise hundreds of feet on all sides of the island. The *ahu* are spaced about one-half mile (805 m) apart, forming a nearly unbroken ring.

Each *ahu* belonged to a family group and was built on the territory where that clan lived. The location of the *ahu* may have marked the boundary between family properties. Some resembled large altars and were

8

Easter Island's ancient writing system is called *rongorongo* and is a kind of picture writing that uses symbols of familiar objects. Only about 20 wooden tablets containing these symbols exist, and the writing has never been **deciphered**. Every other line is upside down, so to read *rongorongo*, the tablets must be turned after each line.

likely used for religious rituals; others were built as burial chambers. The Rapa Nui constructed the *ahu* from slabs of stone that formed the top and outer sides and were supported by rubble or rough-cut stones in the middle. The back of the platform, which faced the sea, was steep; the front, which faced inland, formed a sloping ramp. In front of many of the *ahu* was a kind of stone-paved plaza where people gathered. Some of the *ahu* supported as many as 15 statues in a long line. Others held only one figure. Inland from some of the plazas were boat-shaped, thatched houses where priests who performed the ceremonies likely stayed.

Archaeologists do not yet understand why, but over time, the Rapa Nui carved larger and larger statues. The *moai* that shows the greatest evolution in design and posture depicts a kneeling, bearded figure and may be one of the last statues carved on the island.

Only one moai *(opposite
bottom)*, *which kneels on
the slope of Rano Raraku,
was created with legs.
Other* moai *were erected
in rows on ahu (left).
Besides sculpting these
figures, the Rapa Nui
also carved images of the
birdman into smaller
rocks (opposite center).*

CARVED FROM VOLCANIC ASH

While most moai *were carved from the island's plentiful supply of tuff, others were chiseled from basalt (right). In addition to sculpting rock, the Rapa Nui also carved intricate wooden items representing animals such as lizards and sea slugs (below).*

The *moai* stand guard over the entire island, although most are clustered along the coast. Some statues never made it to their final destination and lay along roads or in and around the Rano Raraku quarry. The quarry provided the Rapa Nui with a ready supply of tuff, or hardened volcanic ash—a soft stone that was easy to carve. About 50 *moai* were carved from other types of rock found elsewhere on the island, including **basalt.**

Rapa Nui sculptors were skilled craftsmen and honored members of the community. Other islanders provided them with food

such as sweet potatoes and fish. Ruins of stone houses near the quarry suggest that the sculptors may have lived there. The sculptors worked with only a few tools made of stone, bone, and **coral.** Archaeologists have found thousands of *toki*—ax-like tools made of basalt—in the quarry. Obsidian was used to make cutting and scraping tools, drills, and files.

The *moai* were carved horizontally out of the sloped quarry walls. Sculptors first chipped the outline of a statue's profile on its side. Then they made a niche around the

The hands of most moai *meet near their navel (right). Besides pieces created for rituals, the Rapa Nui also carved wooden tools, including the* papahia *(below) for pounding food, and wooden ornaments such as breastplates (below right).*

outlined figure so they could chisel from both sides. Sculptors carved the head first and finished with the hips.

No two statues were identical, but most followed a basic model. The *moai* were designed as standing figures ending at the hip. The arms hung straight down, and the long-fingered hands curved around the front of the abdomen. The heads were long and faced forward. Most of the faces had narrow lips, large noses, and deep eye sockets below a high forehead. The ears were typically long and sometimes had depressions in the lobes where ornaments could be inserted.

Once finished, the statues were polished with pieces of coral to produce a smooth, shiny surface. In some cases, the bodies were engraved with elaborate designs that are believed to represent tattoos. Most figures are male in appearance, although a few female examples exist as well.

The size of the statues varied significantly and increased over time. Some are only six feet (1.8 m) tall, but on average, they stand 13.3 feet (4.1 m) tall and weigh 13.8 tons (12.5 t). The heaviest standing *moai*, found near the coast north of Rano Raraku quarry, measures 32 feet (9.7 m) and is estimated to weigh 82 tons

The steep cliffs and strong surf of Easter Island form a stunning backdrop to the moai *that stand in silent watchfulness over the island. A few* moai *face out to sea, but the majority face inland to protect the descendants of their builders.*

Large, triangular wooden sledges may have been used to transport the huge moai. *The difficulties of moving the monuments with sledges may be why some broken* moai *appear to have been abandoned between the quarry and the* ahu.

(74 t). The tallest *moai* still lies in the quarry, attached to its base, and is 71 feet (21 m) long.

After they carved the front of a statue, sculptors undercut the bottom until only a narrow, horizontal ridge of rock attached the statue to the quarry wall. They then cut away this ridge so the *moai* could be lowered to the quarry floor with ropes. There workers set the figure upright into a hole in the ground, enabling sculptors to complete their work on the back. Some 50 to 75 *moai* once had rounded blocks of red stone, called *pukao*, on their

heads. These hats or **topknots** gave the statues extra height and grandeur.

One of the many mysteries surrounding the *moai* is how they were transported to the *ahu*. One legend claims that priests gave special power to the statues so they could walk a short distance each day until they reached the *ahu*. In actuality, the Rapa Nui probably devised some type of **sledge** from the giant palm trees on the island to pull the statues along the many roads leading away from the quarry. When a statue reached its final location, workers probably levered it in stages to a standing position.

Besides the large moai carved from tuff, a few small statues made from red scoria have been found. Red scoria is the same stone that was used for the topknots of the larger moai and came from the Puna Pao quarry, located several miles from the Rano Raraku quarry.

A CULTURE NEARLY DESTROYED

Although Easter Island was once covered in palm trees and food crops such as yams (below), mismanagement of resources led to the destruction of the land. But the island's crater lakes continue to support totora reeds, from which the Rapa Nui make boats (opposite) and other useful items.

The Polynesian seafarers who first settled Easter Island found an island populated only by seabirds nesting in giant palm trees. Eventually, the settlers formed eight separate Rapa Nui groups, each with its own name and territory. As they began the time-consuming task of carving *moai*, the Rapa Nui cleared land to grow crops. To transport the finished statues, they probably chopped down palm trees to make sledges.

Centuries later, in the early 1600s, another group of Polynesians arrived on the small island. Estimates vary, but most historians believe that the island's population grew to between 4,000 and 9,000 inhabitants. Eventually, fighting broke out between clans. As different groups competed for land and resources, the worst offense to another clan was to damage its *ahu* or *moai*. By the late 1600s, all of the island's trees had been cut down. Land **eroded** more quickly without the trees' roots to hold the soil together, making farming difficult.

In 1722, Dutch sailor Jacob Roggeveen became the first nonnative to see the island. He hoped to find food and minerals on the island and to perhaps establish a new trading post. Upon closer inspection, however, he

20

The totora reed is a water plant that grows on Easter Island. The reed had many uses to the Rapa Nui. Bound together, the plant stems could be made into thatch to cover houses. Islanders also used the reed to weave baskets, mats, and small, surfboard-like rafts.

Two English explorers—Katherine Routledge and her husband, William Scoresby Routledge—were the first people to launch a formal scientific expedition on Easter Island. In 1914 and 1915, they talked with the island's natives, examined the statues, collected **artifacts**, and gathered data.

Although many of the statues had fallen before James Cook (right) saw them in 1774, he recognized the ingenuity of their builders.

was disappointed to find a landscape barren of trees and fresh water and a society of people at war. Roggeveen left the island after just two days, but not before naming it Easter Island in honor of the day he landed there: Easter Sunday.

Famous British explorer James Cook reached Easter Island some 50 years later during a voyage through the South Pacific. Clan warfare had increased on the island, and Cook found that many of the statues had been toppled and lay facedown on the ground. By 1863, when **missionaries** arrived on the island, the population had dropped to about 3,000. Around this time,

South American slave raiders took more than 1,000 Rapa Nui to work in **guano** mines in Peru. Most died from exhaustion or smallpox, and the 15 Rapa Nui who returned to Easter Island from Peru brought the smallpox virus with them. By 1877, only about 100 natives remained on the island.

By the time the government of Chile took possession of Easter Island in 1888, all of the *moai* had fallen over. The heads had broken off of many, and some were eroding badly. It wasn't until the early 1900s that outsiders returned, this time to study the mysterious stone **monoliths** and

Although Easter Island's remoteness makes its statues one of the world's least visited ancient wonders, scientists and archaeologists such as Jo Anne Van Tilburg (right) continue to be fascinated by the study of these gigantic monuments.

determine how a once-thriving culture had come to such a tragic end.

While attempting to learn more about the Rapa Nui in the past century, scientists have also undertaken major efforts to identify, restore, and erect the *moai* where they once stood. Between 1969 and 1976, American, British, and Chilean archaeologists excavated and restored many of the *ahu*. From 1982 to 1994, American archaeologist Jo Anne Van Tilburg, the world's leading authority on the *moai*, led a scientific team that measured, mapped, and photographed all of the statues on Easter Island.

Today, much of Easter Island (including all of the major archaeological sites) is des-ignated a Chilean national park; in 1995, the park was named a protected World Heritage Site. Much of the island is now used to raise sheep, producing wool for export. Perhaps encouraged in part by the 1994 movie *Rapa Nui*, about 24,000 people a year visit Easter Island to explore the mysteries of its lonely landscape.

Millions of years ago, a volcanic eruption left a tiny island in the vast blue expanse of the Pacific Ocean. In this most remote of places, a culture took root that produced some of the world's grandest and most fascinating sculptures. Today, the statues of Easter Island stand watch over this mysterious island much as they have for centuries, symbols of a way of life forever lost.

Archaeologists use many different methods to obtain information about the moai. Some methods, such as observing the statues from every angle, are simple. Others, such as placing a grid over the statues to measure them for computer images (top), are more sophisticated.

SEEING THE WONDER

Spanish is the official language of Easter Island today, but the native language, still spoken by some of the islanders, is Rapanui. In Rapanui, the word for "hello" and "good-bye"—*iorana*—is the same.

A visit to Easter Island can provide a glimpse into the history of both its statues and people.

Although Easter Island is very remote and expensive to reach, a visit to its lonely shores is an experience without equal. Most tourists choose to visit the island in December or January (early summer in the southern hemisphere) and arrive by cruise ship or a five-hour flight from Santiago, Chile. Visitors to the island are issued a tourist card that allows them to stay for up to 90 days. Tourists may rent cars, motorcycles, or bicycles to get around the island. Because of the island's small size, many visitors do much of their traveling on foot.

Organized tours led by local guides cost about $40 a day and take visitors to the island's many archaeological sites. Nearly 400 statues can be seen at the Rano Raraku quarry, many still attached to the quarry walls. The impressive Tongariki *ahu*, located in the eastern part of the island, holds 15 standing statues. At the ceremonial site of Orongo, south of the island's capital city of Hanga Roa, are the remains of ancient stone houses and some stunning petroglyphs, or rock carvings. North of Hanga Roa are the Akivi *ahu* and caves that were home to many of the early

2 6

The Tapati Festival is Easter Island's annual celebration, held in late January and early February. Begun in 1975, the festival includes native dancing, chanting, singing, and body decorating; competitions such as horse racing; wood carving and fishing; and a parade.

Besides the *moai*, Easter Island has another distinctive art style called the *moai kavakava*, or "statue of ribs." These wooden figures, carved and sold today by island residents, are said to represent ghosts.

Moai kavakava *(below)* **statues seem to embody the mysteries of Easter Island.**

Rapa Nui. The island's Anakena Beach area features petroglyphs and great swimming.

In Hanga Roa, many visitors explore the Museo Antropológico Sebastián Englert. Named after a Catholic priest who lived on the island from 1935 to 1970 and recorded the Rapa Nui culture, the museum displays statue fragments, ancient wooden tablets, basalt fishhooks, spearheads, and other artifacts. The centerpiece of the exhibit is a coral eye that has sparked debate over whether the *moai* once had inlaid eyes.

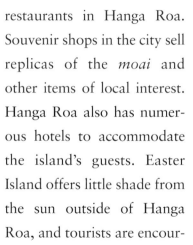

After a day of hiking and viewing the *moai* and *ahu*, visitors may relax and enjoy a meal of fruit juice and fish at one of several restaurants in Hanga Roa. Souvenir shops in the city sell replicas of the *moai* and other items of local interest. Hanga Roa also has numerous hotels to accommodate the island's guests. Easter Island offers little shade from the sun outside of Hanga Roa, and tourists are encouraged to wear a hat and sunscreen and to carry bottles of water. Sturdy shoes are also necessary for navigating the island's rocky terrain.

STATUES OF  EASTER ISLAND

QUICK FACTS

Location: South Pacific Ocean; 2,300 miles (3,680 km) west of Chile

Age: Range from about 1,600 to 350 years old

Land area of Easter Island: 64 square miles (163 sq km)

Number of statues: 887 (including 397 still in the Rano Raraku quarry)

Composition: Hardened volcanic ash

Builders: Rapa Nui sculptors

Average statue dimensions:

Height: 13.3 feet (4.1 m)

Width: 4.9 feet (1.5 m) at head

Weight: 13.8 tons (12.5 t)

First foreigner to view: Dutch sailor Jacob Roggeveen (April 6, 1722)

Geographic setting: Volcanic island

Visitors per year: About 24,000

Native plant life: Almost all native species are extinct and have been replaced by such plants as European grasses, eucalyptus trees, and coconut palms

Native animal life: Seabirds such as the sooty tern, sheep (introduced in the 1900s), flies, cockroaches, spiders, scorpions, and mosquitoes

Other name for Easter Island: *Te Pito o Te Henua*—"The Navel of the World" (name used by Rapa Nui)

GLOSSARY

archaeologists—scientists who learn about the past by digging up and studying old structures or objects

artifacts—objects produced or shaped by humans, especially a tool or ornament of interest to archaeologists

basalt—a hard, dark rock with a glassy appearance; it is formed by volcanic activity

coral—a rock-like substance created by certain marine (sea) organisms

deciphered—figured out so as to be understood

eroded—worn away by wind and water

guano—a substance made up mostly of the dung of seabirds; it can be used as a fertilizer

icons—images or pictures of a sacred person that are important and long-lasting symbols

lineage—a person's family history

missionaries—people who go to a foreign country to spread religion or do charity work

monoliths—large blocks of stone shaped into pillars, statues, or monuments

sledge—a wooden sled pulled across timber rollers to transport heavy objects such as stone sculptures

topknots—crests or knots of hair or feathers on top of a head